D1408564

Knowledge MASTERS plus

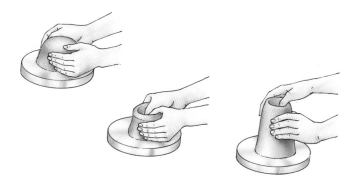

HOW THINGS
ARE MADE

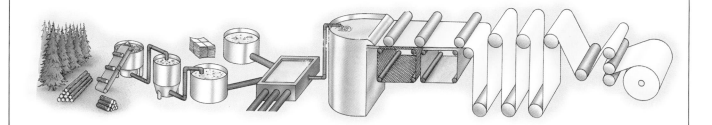

Written by
Peter Lafferty

Consultant
Andrew Woodward

Illustrated by
Jeremy Gower and Mainline Design

zigzag

About this book

Consultant:
Andrew Woodward,
BEng (Hons) MICE,
is a civil engineer
with experience in
many aspects of
construction, and
music technology.

Published in 2002 by
Zigzag, an imprint of
Chysalis Children's
Books,
64 Brewery Road,
London N7 9NT

© 2002 Zigzag
Children's Books

Cover illustrators:
Jeremy Gower
Mainline Design

Cover design:
Nicky Chapman and
Danny McBride

Concept: Tony Potter
Editors: Kay
Barnham
and Hazel Songhurst

Printed and bound in
China.

ISBN 1-903954-38X (HB)
ISBN 1-903954-428 (PB)

INTERNET LINKS
Every effort has been
made to ensure none
of the recommended
websites in this book is
linked to inappropriate
material. However, due
to the ever-changing
nature of the Internet,
the publishers regret
they cannot take
responsibility for
future content of
these websites.

This book explains many different ways of making the things that you see and use every day. Find out how photographs are developed, how skyscrapers are built and how books are printed. These and other fascinating topics are explored in clear text and colourful pictures.

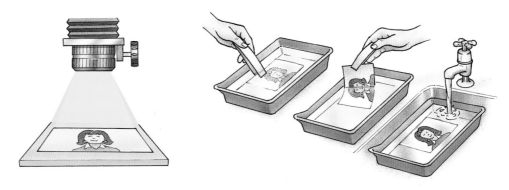

INTERNET SAFETY

Internet Links throughout the book allow you to explore topics further, including history-related activities and games. Be sure to follow these guidelines for a fun and safe journey through cyberspace:

1. Ask your parents for permission before you go online.
2. Spend time with your parents online and show them your favourite sites.
3. Post your family's e-mail address, even if you have your own (only give your personal address to someone you trust).
4. Do not reply to e-mails if you feel they are strange or upsetting.
5. Do not use your real surname while you are online.
6. Never arrange to meet 'cyber friends' in person without your parents' permission.
7. Never give out your password.
8. Never give out your home address or telephone number.
9. Do not send scanned pictures of yourself unless your parents approve.
10. Leave a website straight away if you find something that is offensive or upsetting. Talk to your parents about it.

The illustrated Timeline that runs through the book shows you the developments and inventions that have changed the world from earliest times to the present day.

AD 1779

Englishman Abraham Darby builds the first cast-iron bridge over the River Severn in Shropshire, England.

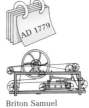

AD 1779

Briton Samuel Crompton invents the spinning mule which can spin 1,000 threads at the same time.

AD 1786

English inventor Edmund Cartwright invents the power loom and revolutionizes the weaving industry.

AD 1792

American Eli Whitney invents the cotton gin which separates cotton fibres from the seeds.

Contents

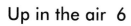

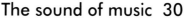
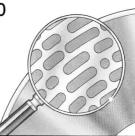

Building a home

A building site is a busy place. Many skilled workers are at work: architects, bricklayers, carpenters, roof tilers, electricians, plumbers. Each person has a special task to carry out.

Foundations

Foundations support the weight of the house. A trench is dug and filled with concrete to make the foundations. The brick walls are built on the foundations.

Building upstairs

Strong timber beams, called joists, are laid from one wall to the other. Wooden floorboards are nailed across the joists to make the floor of an upstairs room. Plasterboard is nailed underneath the joists to make the ceiling of the downstairs room.

Keeping damp out

Just above the ground a waterproof layer is put in the wall. This is called the damp-proof course. It stops water soaking into the walls.

Concrete blocks

Cement mixer

Joists

Foundations

Making plans

The first step in building a house is to draw a plan to show what the house should look like, how many rooms it should have and where they are located. An architect draws the plans after talking to the people who will be living in the house.

The fastest bricklayer in the world is Tony Gregory of Essex, England. In 1987 he laid 747 bricks in one hour.

Building the walls

Bricklayers build the corners of the house first. They stretch string between the corners to help build the walls straight. The inner walls are built from large concrete blocks.

10,000 BC

The earliest stone buildings are built by Stone Age people.

7000 BC

In Iran, simple pottery is shaped by hand from clay.

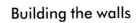

7000 BC

The earliest looms are used to make cloth. One set of threads hangs down from a frame, and the weaver passes other threads between them.

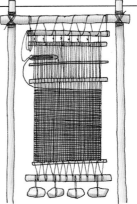

6000 BC

In the Middle East, the first bricks are made from clay baked in the sun.

On top

The roof is held up by wooden frames, called roof trusses, which rest on the wall. The frames are made in a factory and delivered to the building site.

Roofing felt is then stretched over the frames. This makes the roof waterproof.

Strips of wood called battens are laid across the top of the felt and nailed to the frame. They hold the felt in place.

Tiles are nailed to the battens. The tiles are laid in rows, from the bottom upwards. Each row overlaps the tiles below so that rain flows off the roof and does not get under the tiles.

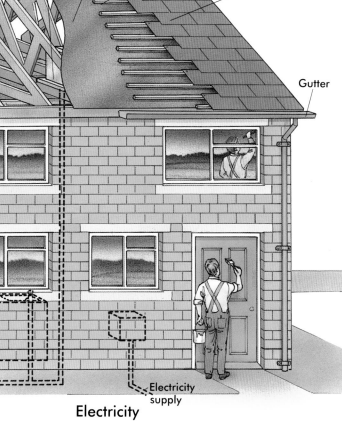

Roof trusses

Water tank

Felt

Battens

Roof tiles

Gutter

Water supply

Electricity supply

Cavity wall

Plumbing

A plumber installs the water and sewage pipes. A pipe, called the water main, carries water into the house. There is a cold water tank in the space under the roof. A hot water tank is fitted in a cupboard. A waste pipe leads the waste water and sewage out of the house.

Electricity

Electricity enters the house through a thick wire called the mains cable. The cable is connected to an electricity meter which measures how much electricity is used. An electrician installs the wires connecting the lights, cookers and sockets to the meter.

Finishing off

To finish off the house, a glazier puts glass in the windows. A plasterer puts a smooth layer of plaster over the walls. A painter and decorator paints the walls, window and door frames. Now the house is ready to live in!

6000 BC

In the Middle East, an alcoholic drink like beer is made from grain.

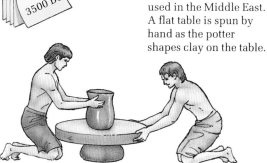

3600 BC

Tin is mixed with copper to make bronze. It makes better tools and weapons.

3500 BC

Egyptians make gold and silver ornaments. They also discover how to make glass.

3500 BC

The potter's wheel is used in the Middle East. A flat table is spun by hand as the potter shapes clay on the table.

Up in the air

Skyscrapers are the giants of the building world. Some are so tall that the weather at the top can be snowy while it is sunny at ground level. These giant buildings must be very strong to stay up.

A strong base

A skyscraper can weigh as much as four large ocean liners. To bear the great weight, the underground foundations need to be strong. To make the foundations, a large pit is dug and filled with concrete. The concrete sets hard and forms a solid base for the building. Some skyscrapers are supported by legs, called piles, of concrete or steel. The piles go deep into the ground.

Building a skyscraper

In one skyscraper design, there is a hollow central tower made of concrete. The elevators and stairs are built inside the tower. The tower stops the building swaying in the wind.

Going higher

A tower crane lifts girders and wall sections up to the top of the building. The crane is fixed to the side of the building to keep it steady.

A trolley moves along the arm of the crane, carrying a load to where it is needed.

A frame of steel girders is built around the tower. The frame supports the floors and walls. The outer walls are made of lightweight material, often glass.

The floors are made by bolting a steel sheet between the girders. Next thin steel rods are laid over the sheet, and concrete poured on. The steel rods strengthen the concrete.

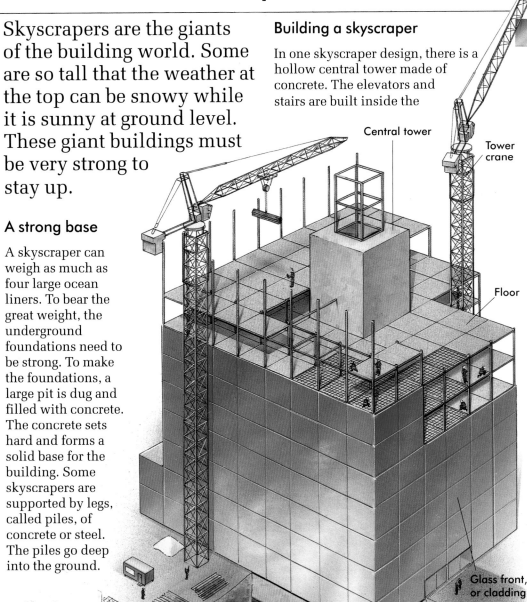

Central tower

Tower crane

Floor

Glass front, or cladding

Foundation Piles

3500 BC

The ancient Egyptians use papyrus reed to make a form of paper. The name 'paper' comes from papyrus.

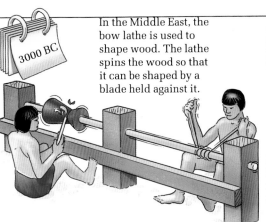

3000 BC

In the Middle East, the bow lathe is used to shape wood. The lathe spins the wood so that it can be shaped by a blade held against it.

2000 BC

Egyptians make sweets by using honey flavoured with juice from the mallow plant.

700 BC

King Ardys of Lydia (now Turkey) issues the first coins made from a mixture of gold and silver.

INTERNET LINK http://www.pbs.org/wgbh/buildingbig
Learn how bridges, tunnels and skyscrapers are built. Then test yourself to see what sort of structure you could build!

Erecting a crane

Tall cranes are used to lift steel girders and wall panels into place. A crane is made of steel sections that are bolted together. The first few sections are placed in position by a mobile crane.

A special section called a climbing frame is placed near the top. The climbing frame is slightly larger than a normal section and has one side open.

Once the crane's hook has been attached at the top, further sections can be lifted into the climbing frame by the crane itself. The climbing frame then moves upwards, making the tower taller.

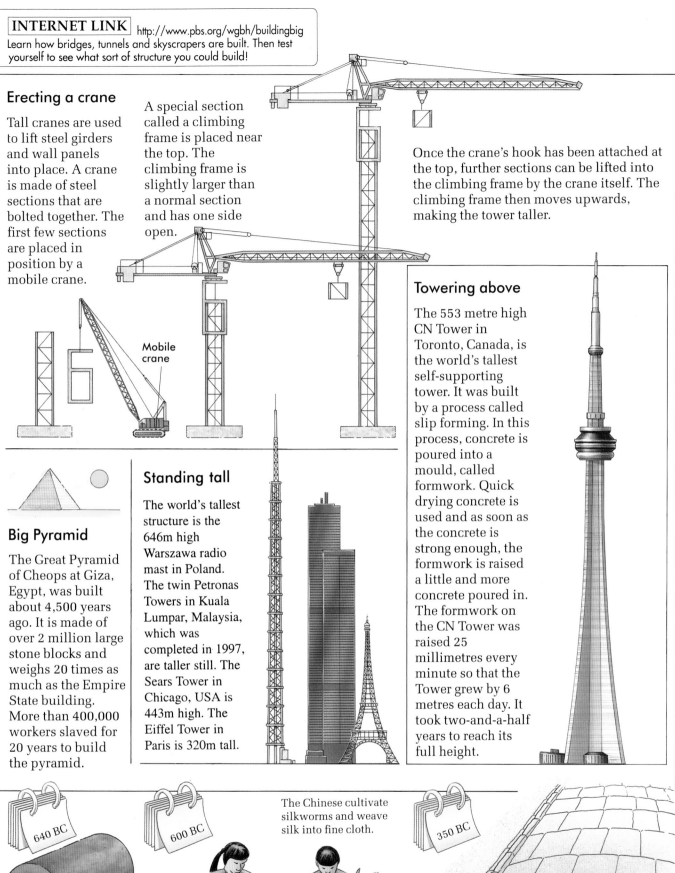

Mobile crane

Towering above

The 553 metre high CN Tower in Toronto, Canada, is the world's tallest self-supporting tower. It was built by a process called slip forming. In this process, concrete is poured into a mould, called formwork. Quick drying concrete is used and as soon as the concrete is strong enough, the formwork is raised a little and more concrete poured in. The formwork on the CN Tower was raised 25 millimetres every minute so that the Tower grew by 6 metres each day. It took two-and-a-half years to reach its full height.

Big Pyramid

The Great Pyramid of Cheops at Giza, Egypt, was built about 4,500 years ago. It is made of over 2 million large stone blocks and weighs 20 times as much as the Empire State building. More than 400,000 workers slaved for 20 years to build the pyramid.

Standing tall

The world's tallest structure is the 646m high Warszawa radio mast in Poland. The twin Petronas Towers in Kuala Lumpar, Malaysia, which was completed in 1997, are taller still. The Sears Tower in Chicago, USA is 443m high. The Eiffel Tower in Paris is 320m tall.

640 BC

The first roof tiles are used on the Temple of Hera at Olympia in Greece.

600 BC

The Chinese cultivate silkworms and weave silk into fine cloth.

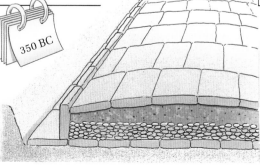

350 BC

The Romans make the first good roads to link parts of their empire.

On the road

Roads changed the way people travel. In the 19th century, before motor vehicles were common, people travelled long distances by rail. Now, motorways connect distant cities and countries, and many people travel by car.

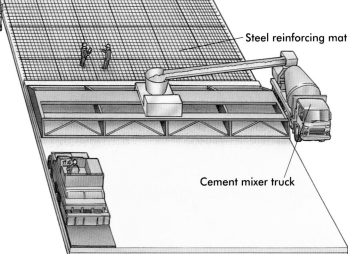

Steel reinforcing mat

Cement mixer truck

Roadmaking

Roads need to be strong, so they are built up from several layers.

To make a motorway, ready-mixed concrete is fed into a paver. This machine puts down an even layer of concrete as it creeps along.

Then a mat of steel reinforcing is laid, followed by another layer of concrete. Finally the road is given a non-skid surface of hot rolled asphalt or rough concrete.

Cars by the million

A car body is made of steel panels. The panels are formed by powerful hydraulic presses. These giant machines are operated by liquids under high pressure. Their precisely shaped jaws press and shape metal with a force of many tonnes.

The panels are welded together by robots on the assembly line. Welding fixes one piece of metal to another piece by using a powerful electric spark. The heat of the spark melts the metal in a precise place.

After building the car bodies, robots fit the doors, the windows and weld the roof in place. They also paint the cars. Then the inside trim and the instruments are put in place.

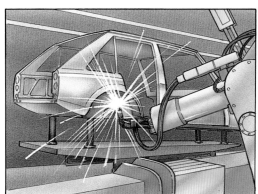

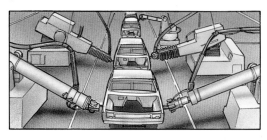

Now, humans fit the engine, the gearbox and the fuel tank. Finally, the radiator, the battery, the springs, the steering and the wheels and tyres are fitted.

50 BC

The Phoenicians in the Middle East are the first people to 'blow' molten glass into jars and other shapes.

10 BC

The first sugar comes from the Far East, possibly from Papua New Guinea.

10 BC

Roman writer Vitruvius describes a crane which can be used to lift heavy weights during building work.

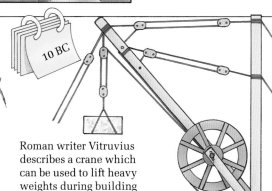

AD 79

Roman carpenters use planes to smooth wooden boards.

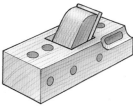

Tunnelling under

Large tunnels are made by a tunnel boring machine or TBM. A driver, guided by a beam of laser light, steers the TBM accurately as it pushes itself forward.

At the front is a cutting head with teeth that bore through the earth and rock.

A long screw carries the waste material back to a conveyor belt. Rail trucks carry it to the surface.

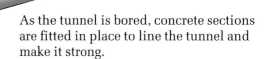

Concrete segments

Conveyor belt

Cutting head

Rail truck

As the tunnel is bored, concrete sections are fitted in place to line the tunnel and make it strong.

Bridging the gap

To make a bridge over a road, thick concrete piers are built. A crane lifts concrete beams which are laid across the piers.

Bridge pier

Bridge beam

Concrete pump

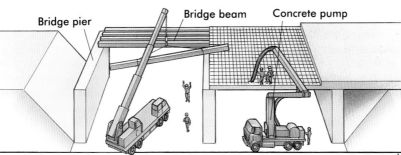

Then reinforcing steel rods are placed on top of the beams. Concrete is poured on top of the rods to make the roadway.

Suspension bridges are very long bridges, suspended from strong cables. First the foundations for the towers are built, and the massive concrete blocks that anchor the cables are put in place.

The towers are constructed and the cables made from bundles of steel wire stretched between the towers.

The deck of the bridge is made from separate massive sections. These are floated to the bridge, lifted into position and hung from the main cables.

Bridge deck

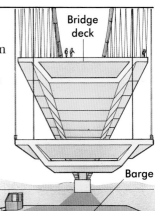

Barge

 AD 105

In China, T'sai Lun makes the first paper from a mixture of cloth, wood and straw. He gets the idea from watching wasps building their nests from chips of wood.

 AD 600

The Chinese issue the first paper money.

AD 865

The first printed book, The Diamond Sutra, is produced in China. The book records the life and teachings of the religious leader, Buddha.

What's cooking?

The largest chocolate bar ever was made by hand in Holland during 1990. It weighed more than 8,000 normal-sized chocolate bars. Ordinary chocolate bars may be smaller than the record-breaking bar, but there are more of them! They are made in factories by the million every day.

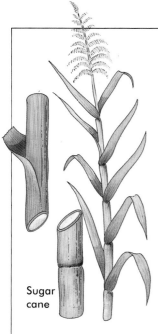

Sugar cane

Sugar, sugar

Most sugar is made from the juice squeezed from sugar cane. The juice is boiled and then spun in a revolving drum like a spin drier to remove water. Crystals of brown sugar are left behind in the drum. Brown sugar is washed, bleached, dissolved in water, filtered and then crystallised again to make white sugar.

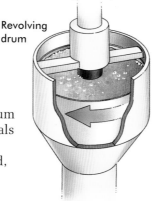

Revolving drum

Making chocolate

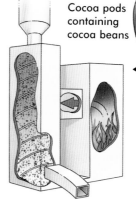

Cocoa pods containing cocoa beans

◀ Chocolate is made from cocoa beans which grow in South America and Africa. When the beans arrive at the chocolate factory, they are cleaned and roasted.

The inside of the bean, called the nib, is separated from the husk or outer layer. The nibs are then ground to make a paste. ▶

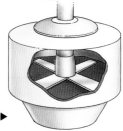

◀ This paste is mixed with sugar, fat and other ingredients. It is heated and stirred to form a smooth, creamy liquid.

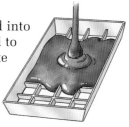

The liquid is poured into moulds and allowed to set to make chocolate bars. When the bars are cool they are wrapped. ▶

Sometimes a centre is placed in a mould that already has a coating of chocolate. More liquid chocolate is then is poured in to cover the centre.

Moulds for sweets

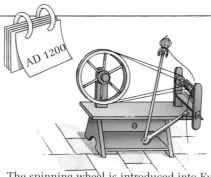

Sweets to suck and chew

Boiled sweets such as barley sugar and hard mints, are made by boiling sugar and water together. Flavours and colouring are then added. The thick syrup which is produced is put into moulds and cooled. Chewy sweets, such as toffees and caramels, are made by boiling sugar and milk together until the mixture turns brown. Butter is also added to give the sweets extra flavour.

AD 1040

In China, Pi Sheng invents printing using movable type. The type had a single character carved on it.

AD 1200

The spinning wheel is introduced into Europe from India. It is used to draw out the wool and spin it into a fine thread.

AD 1267

A C D

British scientist Roger Bacon experiments with lenses, making a magnifying glass.

AD 1300

Crown glass is first used in Europe to make window panes.

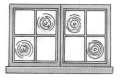

Freezing food

Food is frozen in a factory using a large, very cold freezer. Inside, the temperature is twice as cold as the freezer compartment of a household refrigerator. The food travels around a long spiral conveyor belt until it is completely frozen.

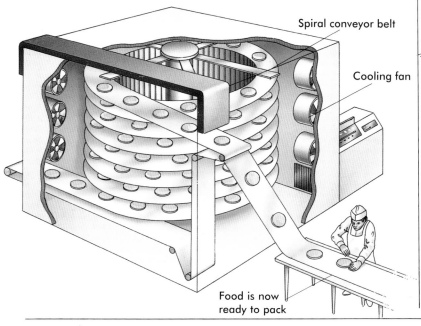

Spiral conveyor belt

Cooling fan

Food is now ready to pack

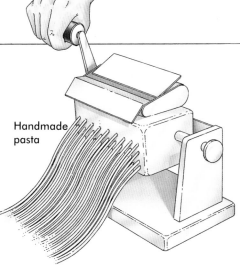

Handmade pasta

Making pasta

'Pasta' is Italian for paste. It is made from wheat which has been coarsely ground and mixed with water. In a spaghetti factory, the paste is squeezed by a screw, like the one in the middle of a mincer, and forced through tiny holes. It emerges as long strands of spaghetti. A knife cuts the strands into equal lengths. The spaghetti is hung on rods to dry and harden.

Fish fingers

1. Fish are fed through a machine with blades that cut a slice of flesh (a fillet) from each side of the fish.

2. The fillets are mixed with other minced fish, pressed into blocks, frozen and then chopped into fingers.

3. The fingers are coated with sticky batter made of flour and water. Then they are covered with bread crumbs.

4. The fingers are briefly fried in hot oil before being quickly refrozen with a blast of freezing-cold air.

5. Machinery packs the fingers at a rate of 2,000 per minute into cartons which are automatically sealed and wrapped.

Raw fish   Chopped   Battered   Breaded   Fried   Re-frozen   Packaged

Minced, pressed and frozen

AD 1316

In Italy, spectacles are first used to improve the sight of short-sighted people.

AD 1454

Johann Gutenberg, a German, invents a printing press. He also invents a mould to make separate metal letters so they can be used over and over again.

AD 1502

Christopher Columbus takes cocoa beans from Mexico to Spain.

AD 1508

Italian painter and scientist Leonardo da Vinci describes how a lens could be fitted directly on to the surface of the eye to correct poor eyesight.

11

Thirsty work

On a hot day, there's nothing better than a cold drink. A fizzy drink is full of bubbles that go up your nose. But how do the bubbles get into the drink? Perhaps you like to drink milk or orange juice? Your parents might prefer coffee or beer. How are these drinks made?

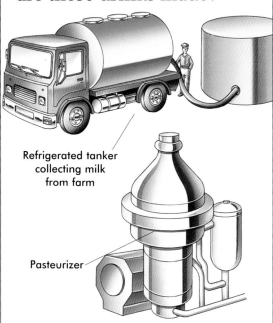

Refrigerated tanker collecting milk from farm

Pasteurizer

Making milk safe

Refrigerated tankers collect milk from the farm and take it to the dairy. At the dairy, the milk is heated for 15 seconds and then quickly cooled. This process is called pasteurization. It kills harmful germs in the milk. Pasteurized milk will stay fresh for longer than untreated milk.

Plenty of fizz

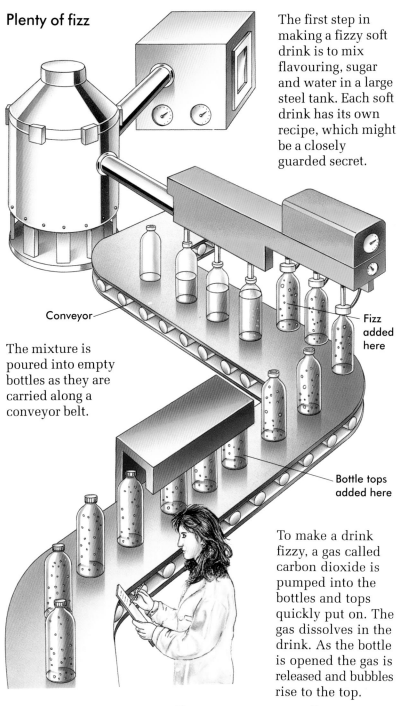

The first step in making a fizzy soft drink is to mix flavouring, sugar and water in a large steel tank. Each soft drink has its own recipe, which might be a closely guarded secret.

Conveyor

Fizz added here

The mixture is poured into empty bottles as they are carried along a conveyor belt.

Bottle tops added here

To make a drink fizzy, a gas called carbon dioxide is pumped into the bottles and tops quickly put on. The gas dissolves in the drink. As the bottle is opened the gas is released and bubbles rise to the top.

AD 1570

The Spanish ambassador to the French court invents the toothbrush.

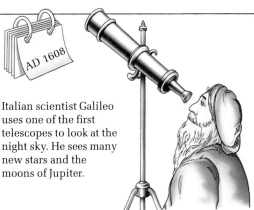

AD 1608

Italian scientist Galileo uses one of the first telescopes to look at the night sky. He sees many new stars and the moons of Jupiter.

AD 1661

The first European banknotes are issued by the Bank of Stockholm, Sweden.

AD 1665

British scientist Robert Hooke makes the first modern microscope using two lenses.

INTERNET LINK http://www.moomilk.com
Take the virtual dairy factory tour and find out more about the story of milk. With fun recipes, puzzles and the moomilk quiz!

A cup of coffee

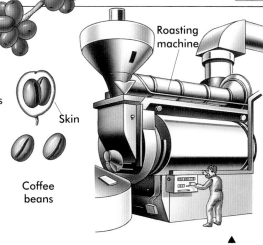

Ripe coffee cherries

Skin

Coffee beans

Roasting machine

The coffee plant grows in Brazil, Columbia, Kenya and India. The coffee berries, often called cherries, are dark red when ripe. After harvesting, the ripe cherries are spread on the ground to dry in the sun. A machine is then used to remove the outer layer of the cherry, leaving the inner part called the bean.

Beans from several places are usually mixed to produce the best combination or blend of flavours. The beans are then roasted in heated spinning drums to bring out the flavour. Coffee beans are sold whole or ground into a powder called ground coffee. Ground coffee can be made into a drink using a machine called a percolator or a special jug called a cafetière.

Instant coffee is made by brewing ground coffee in a giant percolator. The coffee liquid produced is sprayed into a chamber through which hot air is blown. The water in the droplets evaporates, leaving granules of solid coffee. The coffee granules are packed in air-tight containers as quickly as possible to preserve the flavour.

Giant percolator

Barley into beer

Barley

Modern brewery, where beer is made

Barley is the sixth largest food crop – but almost none of it is eaten. Most is made into beer. To turn barley into beer, barley grains are moistened with water and allowed to sprout. Sprouted barley is called malt. The malt is then soaked in warm water and the liquid, called wort, is drained off.

The wort is boiled with flowers from the hop plant to give it a bitter flavour. It is then cooled and yeast is added. Yeasts are microscopic organisms related to fungi. The yeast turns the sugars in the liquid to alcohol. This process is called fermentation and takes up to six days.

After fermentation, the beer is stored in tanks for up to three months to improve the flavour. Then it is strained or spun in a cylinder called a centrifuge to remove the yeast cells. It may then be pasteurized by heating to give the beer a longer life. It is then put into casks, bottles or cans, ready to drink.

AD 1668

English scientist Isaac Newton builds the first telescope using a mirror to collect light.

AD 1683

Dutchman Anton van Leeuwenhoek uses a simple microscope – a single powerful lens – to discover bacteria and blood cells.

AD 1741

Fizzy mineral water is invented by William Browning in Whitehaven, Cumbria, England. He adds bubbles to spring water for extra sparkle.

13

Warm and comfortable

It is said that Mary, Queen of Scots, slept in sheets made from stinging nettles. The fibres or strands of the nettle stems were spun into threads and woven into fine material. Many other materials can also be made into cloth.

Different fibres

Most furry animals produce fibres that can be made into cloth. Wool from sheep was probably the first fibre to be woven into cloth, but goat and rabbit hair can also be used. Silk thread is spun by silkworms.

Plant fibres, too, can be made into cloth. Cotton, flax, and jute are made from plants. There are also synthetic fibres made from chemicals. These include nylon, polyester and acrylic. These are cheaper and stronger than natural fibres.

Wool

Cotton

Flax

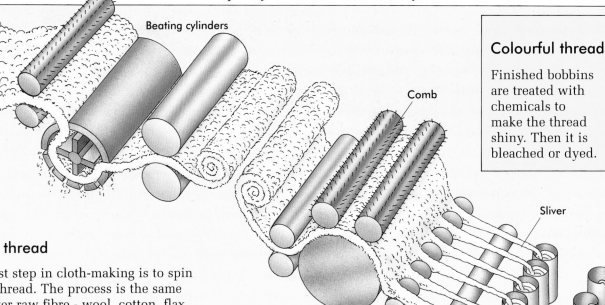

Beating cylinders

Comb

Sliver

Colourful thread

Finished bobbins are treated with chemicals to make the thread shiny. Then it is bleached or dyed.

A fine thread

The first step in cloth-making is to spin a fine thread. The process is the same whatever raw fibre - wool, cotton, flax, or silk - is used.

1. First of all, the raw fibre is cleaned thoroughly. Then it is made into a thick mat by passing it between rollers called beating cylinders.

2. The fibres are combed, or carded, by large rollers covered with wire teeth, to untangle the fibres so that they all lie in the same direction.

3. Slivers, or loose ropes of yarn, are drawn between rollers. The slivers are twisted and stretched to produce a strong, thin thread.

4. Several threads of yarn are twisted together to make the finished piece of thread. The thread is wound onto a bobbin or large reel.

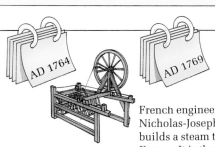

AD 1764

British inventor James Hargreaves builds the spinning jenny – a mechanical spinning machine.

AD 1769

French engineer Nicholas-Joseph Cugnot builds a steam tractor in France. It is the first self-propelled vehicle and is used to tow guns.

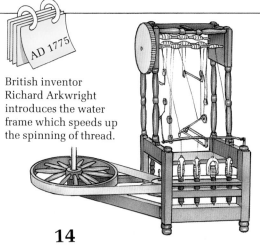

AD 1775

British inventor Richard Arkwright introduces the water frame which speeds up the spinning of thread.

AD 1779

American Benjamin Franklin makes the first bifocal spectacles, combining two types of lens in one frame. The spectacles improve both long and short sight.

The long hair of the angora goat makes warm sweaters. The hair from the angora rabbit, a native of the island of Madeira, is used to make jackets and coats.

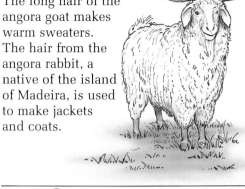

Manmade thread can be mixed with natural thread here to make the thread stronger or easier to wash.

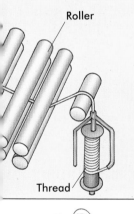

Roller

Thread

Factory weaving

Modern factory looms are completely automated. They automatically add new thread when it runs out, and most machines have no shuttle.

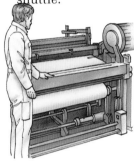

Instead, the weft is put in place by a thin wire with an eyelet at one end, or by a jet of water or air. Newer shuttleless looms are quieter than older machines.

Weaving by hand

Woven cloth is made up of lengthways threads (called warp threads) and crossways threads (called weft threads). A simple hand loom has two light bars, called heddle shafts, carrying fine wire loops through which the warp threads pass.

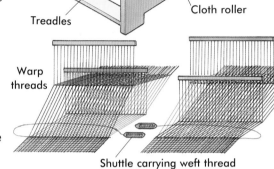

Heddle shaft

Treadles

Cloth roller

Warp threads

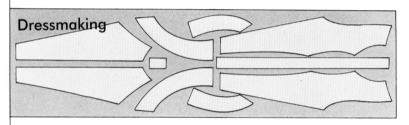

Shuttle carrying weft thread

By pressing on the treadle, the warp threads are parted, with some being pulled upwards and others being pushed downwards. This makes a gap through which the shuttle, carrying the weft thread, can pass. The weft is pushed firmly into the cloth by the reed, a screen made of wire. Pressing another treadle reverses the positions of the warp threads and the shuttle passes back to its original position. The shuttle is passed back and forth many times to weave the cloth.

Dressmaking

To make a dress, the dressmaker uses a paper pattern. The pattern shows which shapes of cloth are needed to make up the dress. Then the pieces of cloth are sewn together using sewing machines. Buttonholes can also be stitched by machine. Finally, the dress is pressed to put creases and pleats into the cloth.

AD 1779

Englishman Abraham Darby builds the first cast-iron bridge over the River Severn in Shropshire, England.

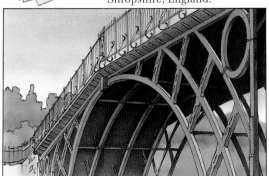

AD 1779

Briton Samuel Crompton invents the spinning mule which can spin 1,000 threads at the same time.

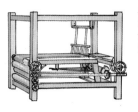
AD 1786

English inventor Edmund Cartwright invents the power loom and revolutionizes the weaving industry.

AD 1792

American Eli Whitney invents the cotton gin which separates cotton fibres from the seeds.

15

Perfectly clear

Glass is one of the oldest artificial materials. In the Middle East around 5,000 years ago, craftsmen made small glass beads to imitate precious gems.

Blowing bottles

A metal mould is used to make a bottle. A lump of molten glass, called a gob, is dropped into the mould and pressed to the bottom by compressed air.

More compressed air is blown in at the bottom to force the glass into the shape of the mould. The rough bottle is then taken out, ready to put into another mould.

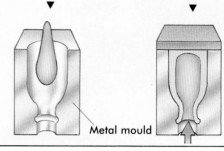

Metal mould

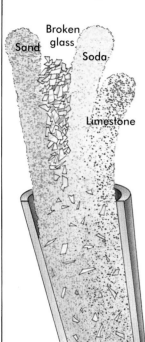

Sand
Broken glass
Soda
Limestone

What is glass made from?

Glass is made from one of the cheapest materials on Earth – sand. The sand is mixed with soda (sodium carbonate), limestone (calcium carbonate) and broken glass (called cullet). The mixture is then heated in a furnace until it melts and makes liquid glass. Special substances may be added to colour the glass or to improve its quality. Adding lead oxide, for example, makes a glass with a brilliant glitter, called crystal glass.

Floating glass

First, the ingredients are heated to a temperature of about 1500°C by flames blowing from the sides of the furnace. To make large sheets of glass, molten glass is poured onto the surface of a bath of molten tin. As it floats on top of the tin, the glass cools and sets, forming a smooth sheet.

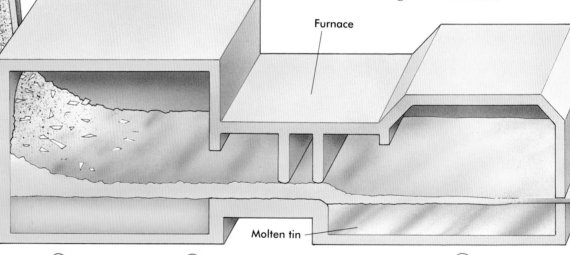

Furnace

Molten tin

AD 1795

French chemist Nicolas Conté makes the first wood-covered pencils.

AD 1797

British engineer Henry Maudslay invents the metal-working lathe to shape metal.

AD 1801

The Jacquard loom, which could weave patterns into cloth or carpet, is invented by Frenchman Joseph Jacquard.

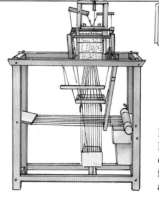

AD 1804

French chef Nicolas-François Appert develops a technique for preserving food in air-tight bottles.

Crown glass

The old way of making window panes was first to blow a large glass bubble using a punty (a sort of iron straw). The bubble was then flattened and spun on the end of the punty. The glass spread out to form a round pane, called crown glass. The crown is the dimple in the centre of the pane.

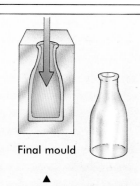

Final mould

▲

Air is blown into the top of the bottle through a tube to form the final shape. The bottle is taken from the mould and allowed to cool and harden.

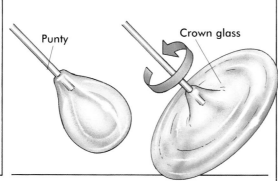

Punty

Crown glass

Stronger than steel

Glass can be drawn into fine threads that are five times stronger than steel. The threads are made by forcing molten glass through fine holes. These fine threads are cooled and wound onto spools.

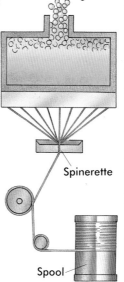

Spinerette

Spool

Glass fibre has many uses. When mixed with plastic, it produces a strong, light material - called glass reinforced plastic, or GRP - that is made into boat hulls and car bodies.

Handmade glass

The oldest way to shape glass objects is by blowing. Some glassware is still made this way. A glass blower dips a hollow iron tube, called a punty, into molten glass and gathers up a blob of glass. The blob is roughly shaped by rolling it on a piece of flat wood.

The glass is then reheated and air is blown down the punty to make a bubble. The punty is turned as the bubble is blown and special tools used to shape the hot glass. When the object is finished, it is cooled slightly and then broken off the punty.

When the glass has cooled enough, it is lifted onto rollers and travels into a cooling chamber, called a lehr. Here the temperature is carefully controlled so that the glass cools slowly and does not crack. It is then cut into sheets by a diamond-tipped cutter and washed with jets of water.

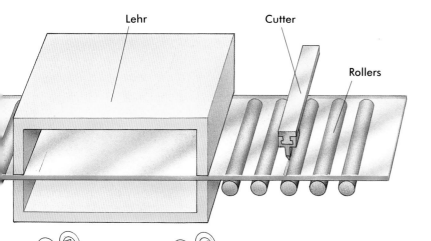

Lehr

Cutter

Rollers

AD 1810

Food is first preserved in tin cans by Englishmen Bryan Donkin and John Hall in their factory in London.

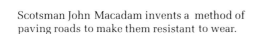

AD 1815

Scotsman John Macadam invents a method of paving roads to make them resistant to wear.

AD 1818

English engineer Marc Brunel builds the first tunnelling machine to tunnel under the River Thames in London.

Pottery and pots

Cups, saucers and teapots are made from mud. This is a special kind of mud, called clay. The clay is shaped and hardened by baking it in an oven. Then it is covered with a waterproof glass-like layer called a glaze.

Getting clay ready

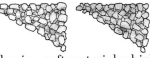

Clay is a soft material which comes in various colours such as white, terracotta and buff. Two kinds of clay used to make pottery are earthenware clay and stoneware clay. China clay is sometimes used, but it is more expensive. Slip, which is a liquid made from clay and water, is used to make hollow pots such as teapots.

Making a vase

1. The first step is to make a model vase. ►

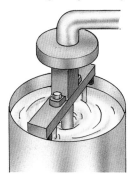
Model vase

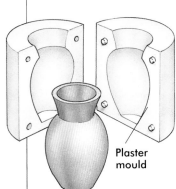
Plaster mould

▲

2. Plaster is poured over this model and allowed to set hard to make a two-piece mould. (It is important to fill vases with clay first to stop plaster running inside.)

3. Slip, a mixture of clay and water, is poured into the mould. Some water soaks into the plaster and the clay around the edge starts to dry out and harden.

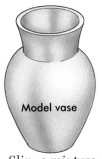
Slip
▼

4. When the layer is thick enough, the remaining slip is poured away. The mould is opened and the vase is taken out.
▼

▲

5. The vase is hardened by baking or 'firing' it in a kiln. Factory kilns are long ovens shaped like a tunnel. The pottery moves down the tunnel on trolleys. This is called bisque firing.

6. Glaze is sprayed onto the vase. The glaze can be clear or coloured.

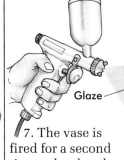
Glaze

7. The vase is fired for a second time to harden the glaze and make the vase waterproof.

AD 1819

A 23-year-old Swiss François-Louis Caliller makes the first bars of chocolate.

AD 1822

Frenchman Joseph Nicephore Niépce takes a photograph with a pinhole camera. Unfortunately the subject has to stay still for 8 hours.

AD 1826

John Walker of Stockton-on-Tees, England, invents the friction match which lights when rubbed on a rough surface.

AD 1828

Dutchman Conraad van Houten first uses cocoa powder to make a hot drink.

INTERNET LINK http://www.ncpotterycenter.com/kids.htm
Learn more about the history of pottery and check out some cool kids'
exhibits, quizzes and contests.

Making a plate

Plates and saucers are made from solid body clay. A pancake of clay is put on a plaster mould shaped like one side of a plate. The mould and clay are pressed against a heated metal tool shaped like the other side of the plate. The clay is squeezed into a plate shape and the excess scraped off.

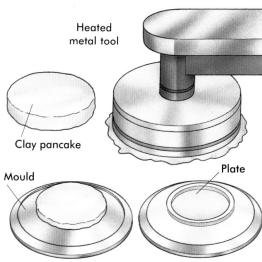

Heated metal tool

Clay pancake

Mould

Plate

Making a cup

Cups are made with a mould. A lump of body clay is placed in the mould and forced against the side by a rotating metal tool.

Mould

The potter's wheel

A potter uses a rapidly turning wheel to shape clay into a pot. This is called 'throwing' a pot. A lump of clay is placed in the centre of the wheel and lubricated with water. The potter uses his hands to draw up the edges of the clay as the wheel turns. As the clay is drawn higher, it forms the sides of the pot.

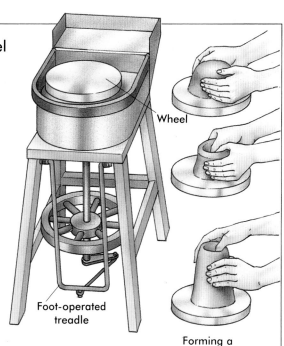

Wheel

Foot-operated treadle

Forming a clay pot

Decorating pottery

Pottery is often decorated with coloured patterns or designs. Designs can be painted on by hand, but more often pottery is screen printed or transfers used. After decorating, the pottery is fired again at a lower temperature to fix the decorations into the glaze. For complicated hand painted designs pottery can be refired several times.

Largest pot

The largest pot made on a wheel measured over 5 metres in height and weighed 600 kilograms. It was made in 1991 by Faiarte Ceramics of Rustenburg, South Africa.

AD 1829

Frenchman Jacques Daguerre invents a method of photography which is much quicker and produces a sharper picture than earlier methods.

AD 1830

The sewing machine is invented by Barthélémy Thimonnier. It can make 200 stitches a minute.

AD 1839

Scot Kirkpatrick Macmillan builds the first bicycle.

Plastics

If everything which contained plastic suddenly vanished from your house, what would be left? Not much! Almost everything in the house contains some plastic materials: soft drink bottles, records, house gutters, garden hosepipes, floor tiles, curtain rails, door and window hinges, cushion filling, electric switches, pan handles.

Making plastics

Plastics are made in chemical factories. Raw materials extracted from oil or coal are heated until they form a sticky liquid. The liquid is then cooled until it sets solid. The solid material is chopped into small lumps called granules. The granules are used to make many different things.

Big molecules

Everything is made up of tiny particles called atoms. In most materials, the atoms form groups called molecules. Most molecules are made up of small numbers of atoms but plastics molecules contain thousands of atoms

Polymer molecule

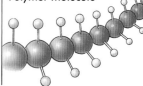

Make your own plastic

Heat some creamy milk in a saucepan. When it is almost boiling, stir in vinegar. Keep stirring until the milk turns solid and rubbery – this is a type of plastic. When it has cooled, wash your plastic under the tap.

Making a toy car

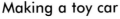

Granules

Injection moulding is a process used to make plastic items such as cups, saucers, bowls, bicycle helmets, saucepan handles and toys. This is how a toy car is made:

Granules of plastic are fed into a moulding machine through a hopper. A ram pushes the granules through the machine. Then, the granules are heated and become soft.

This soft plastic is forced into a steel mould shaped like a small car. The plastic cools and hardens in the shape of the mould. The mould is opened and the car falls out.

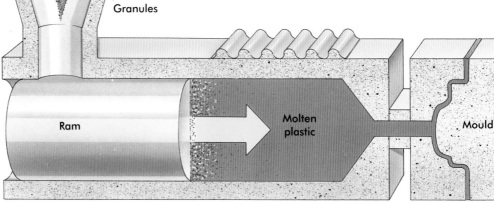

Ram

Molten plastic

Mould

AD 1850

Americans Elias Howe and Isaac Singer perfect the sewing machine.

AD 1850

English engineer Robert Stephenson builds the first box girder bridge over the Menai Straight in Wales.

AD 1855

Mr Yates, a British inventor, makes the first can opener.

AD 1856

First synthetic dye is prepared by English chemist William Perkin.

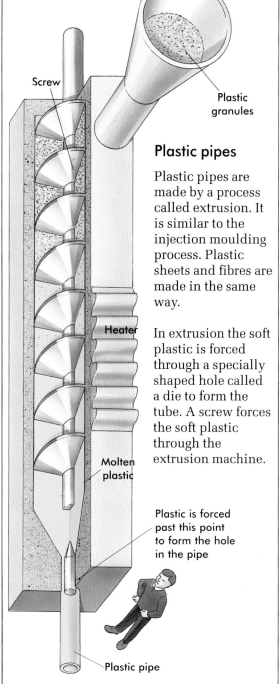

INTERNET LINK http://www.teachingtools.com/slinky/plastics.html
What are plastics? How are they made? Find the answers to these questions and more, and then perform a science experiment.

Blowing bottles

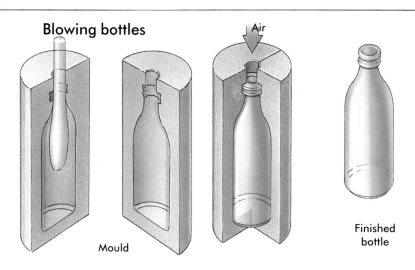

Air

Mould

Finished bottle

Soft plastic is fed into a bottle-shaped mould. Compressed air is blown into the middle of the plastic. The plastic is forced against the walls of the mould, taking a bottle shape. An empty space is left in the centre. When the plastic has set hard, the mould is opened and the bottle taken out. This process is called blow moulding. It is used to make cans, drums, tanks and toys.

Sucked into shape

Vacuum mould for making plastic baths

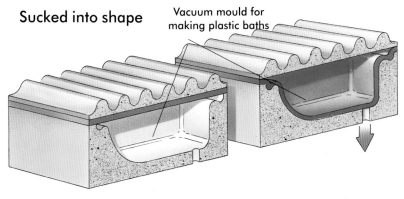

To make a plastic bath, a sheet of plastic is put over a mould. A heater softens the sheet. Air is sucked out of the mould by a vacuum pump. The softened plastic is sucked into the mould, and presses against the sides of the mould. The plastic cools and hardens. The bath is taken out of the mould. This process is called vacuum forming. It is used to make chocolate box liners and throw-away plastic cups.

Plastic pipes

Screw

Plastic granules

Plastic pipes are made by a process called extrusion. It is similar to the injection moulding process. Plastic sheets and fibres are made in the same way.

Heater

In extrusion the soft plastic is forced through a specially shaped hole called a die to form the tube. A screw forces the soft plastic through the extrusion machine.

Molten plastic

Plastic is forced past this point to form the hole in the pipe

Plastic pipe

AD 1856

British industrialist Henry Bessemer makes a converter for producing cheap steel.

AD 1860

Louis Pasteur discovers how to destroy germs in milk by heating it.

AD 1860

Belgian engineer Étienne Lenoir builds the first internal combustion engine. It works like a steam engine, but runs on fuel.

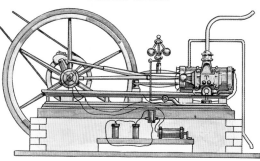

Iron and steel

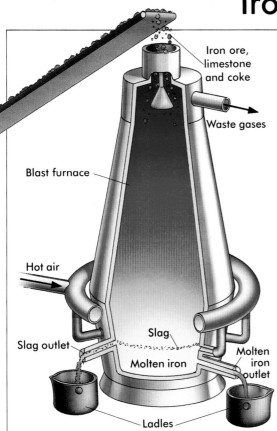

Iron ore, limestone and coke

Waste gases

Blast furnace

Hot air

Slag

Slag outlet

Molten iron

Molten iron outlet

Ladles

Iron was used by some of the earliest civilizations, over 3,000 years ago. Today, it is still the most important metal. Most iron is converted into steel, and made into cars, engines, railway tracks, building girders, pins and needles, food cans and many other things.

Iron to steel

Steel is made by removing most of the carbon from iron which is produced in a blast furnace. This is done in a basic oxygen furnace. Molten iron and scrap steel is put into the furnace and a jet of oxygen is blown into the mixture. The oxygen removes most of the carbon from the iron, converting the iron to steel. When the process is complete, the furnace is tilted and the steel poured into a ladle. One furnace can produce about 500 tonnes of steel in an hour.

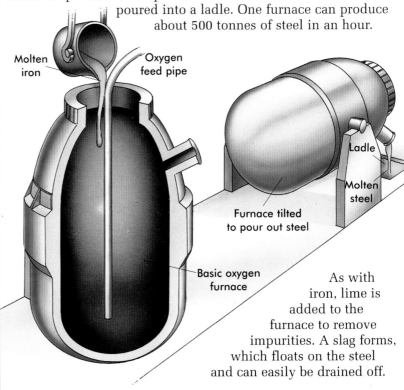

Molten iron

Oxygen feed pipe

Ladle

Molten steel

Furnace tilted to pour out steel

Basic oxygen furnace

Iron works

Iron is extracted from iron ore (a kind of rock) in a blast furnace, a tall cylindrical furnace lined with heat-resistant bricks. The ore is put into the furnace with limestone and coke. A blast of hot air is blown in at the bottom. This heats the raw materials and the coke combines with the ore, releasing liquid iron.

The iron sinks to the bottom of the furnace and flows out into ladles. The limestone combines with unwanted sand and stones in the ore to form a waste material, called slag. The slag floats on top of the molten iron and is easily removed.

As with iron, lime is added to the furnace to remove impurities. A slag forms, which floats on the steel and can easily be drained off.

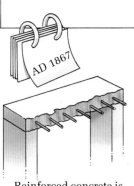

AD 1867

Reinforced concrete is developed by Frenchman Joseph Monier.

AD 1868

In France, Ernest and Pierre Michaux build the first motorcycle.

AD 1876

Ketchup, or tomato sauce, is invented by American Henry Heinz.

AD 1877

Thomas Edison, the American inventor, makes the first phonograph. His invention records sounds on a revolving wax cylinder.

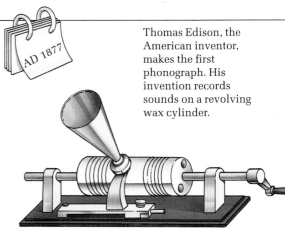

INTERNET LINK http://www.howstuffworks.com/iron.htm
Find out more about refining iron and steel at this popular kids' website.
There are loads of cool animations and games too.

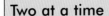

Can it!

Most food cans are made from tinplate which is steel sheet coated with a thin layer of tin. The tin layer stops the can from rusting. Most soft drink cans are made from aluminium which is light and does not rust.

The tinplate is first covered with a layer of lacquer (a kind of clear paint). This protects the tinplate and stops the contents becoming contaminated by the metal.

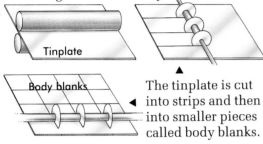

Tinplate

Body blanks

◄ The tinplate is cut into strips and then into smaller pieces called body blanks.

The blanks are then bent around to form a cylinder and the edges joined by heat fusion. This means that the edges are heated and pressed together until they melt and join.

▼

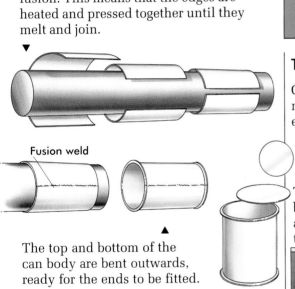

Fusion weld

▲

The top and bottom of the can body are bent outwards, ready for the ends to be fitted.

Two at a time

Needles are made in pairs! Wire is drawn out to the correct thickness and cut to size. The lengths of wire are sharpened at both ends.

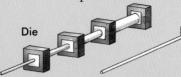

Die

Cutter

Sharpening rollers

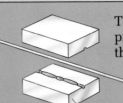

The eyes of the needles are formed by a press which shapes the eyes and punches the holes through.

Press

The needles are separated and unwanted metal ground away. They are then plated with nickel which produces a silvery surface and stops rusting.

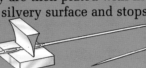

Removing rough edges, or burrs

Tops and bottoms

Can ends are cut from tinplate by a stamping machine called a press. The can bottom's edge is curled over and sealant spread on it.

Then, a machine bends the edge of the bottom over the edge of the can body (1) and squeezes them together (2) to form a tight join which is called a double seam (3).

1   2   3

Testing the can

Finally, the cans are tested to check they do not leak, before they are filled with food and the tops fitted.

AD 1884

American insurance salesman Lewis Waterman makes the first workable fountain pen.

AD 1884

The first skyscraper, the Home Insurance Building in Chicago, is designed by William Le Baron Jenney.

German Karl Benz produces the first petrol-powered motor car.

AD 1885

23

Small wonders

A match is a small everyday item which is often taken for granted. But, like the teabag and the coin, we use millions of them each day. They are as vital to our lives as larger more obvious things.

The jingle in your pocket

The first stage in making a coin is to make a large model showing the design of the coin. The model is made of plaster and is about 300 millimetres across. A smaller steel copy of the model is then made. This copy is pressed into another block of steel to make a die. The die is like a coin with its design reversed; where the coin design has a hollow, the die has a bump.

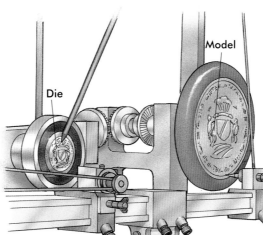

Die

Model

The blanks are next fed into the coining press where each blank is squeezed between two dies. The pressure used is the same as the weight of 30 elephants. This presses the design on the die onto the blank. The coins are then ejected into a container and are inspected carefully. A 'telling' machine counts the coins into bags before they are sent to the banks.

The next stage is to prepare coin-size metal discs called blanks. These are cut from a sheet of metal by a machine called a press. The blanks then pass through a rimming machine to slightly increase the thickness of the coin's edges, or rims. The blanks are then annealed, or softened, by passing through a furnace, and cleaned in an bath of acid.

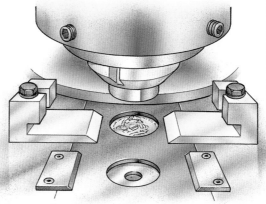

Keep smiling

Toothpaste is a mixture of ten or more ingredients. The main ingredient in the white part of toothpaste is finely powdered chalk which polishes the teeth. Most toothpastes also include fluoride, flavouring and a germicide to kill germs. The ingredients are thoroughly mixed and put into the tube by a machine.

There are two ways of putting coloured stripes in toothpaste. Sometimes the white and coloured pastes are put into the tube separately, and come out together when the tube is squeezed. Another method is to put the coloured paste in a ring near the tube nozzle. The coloured paste is forced through holes to make the stripes when the tube is squeezed.

George Eastman invents the roll film and a simple camera, the Kodak Box Brownie.

Emile Berliner, a German living in America, has the idea of replacing the cylinder used in the first gramophones with a revolving disc.

The German eye specialist Adolf Flick makes moulds of the eyes of corpses to help make the first contact lenses.

Scottish inventor John Dunlop produces the inflatable tyre for his son's bicycle. The tyres make riding more comfortable.

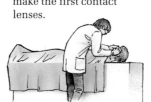

Strike a light

Matches are made by automatic machines that can produce up to 2 million matches per hour. The matchsticks are first cut from a log; one tree provides the wood for a million matches! At the factory, the matchsticks are pushed into holes in a long, moving belt. One end of each matchstick is dipped into paraffin wax. The wax helps the match to burn after it has been lit.

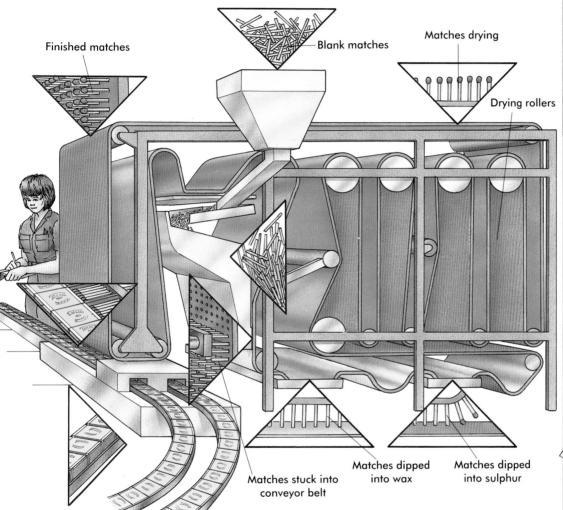

Finished matches — Blank matches — Matches drying — Drying rollers — Matches stuck into conveyor belt — Matches dipped into wax — Matches dipped into sulphur

Next, the ends are dipped into the mixture that coats the match head. The mixture contains sulphur to create the flame and other chemicals to supply oxygen. The matches are slowly dried as the belt moves back and forth past fans. When the heads have dried, the sticks are knocked from the belt into match boxes.

A nice cup of tea

A teabag is not made of ordinary paper. It has to be strong, yet full of holes! Teabag paper is a mixture of two fibres: hemp (which is used to make rope) and plastic fibres. The paper goes through the teabag machine in two strips. A portion of tea is placed on the lower strip and the upper strip is pressed down over the tea. The bag is sealed by heating it around the edges. The plastic in the paper melts and acts like glue to join the strips together.

AD 1889

The Eiffel Tower is designed and built in Paris by French engineer Gustave Eiffel.

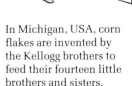

AD 1892

Coca-Cola is invented in the USA by Dr Pemberton. It contains 15 secret ingredients including the still-secret 'ingredient 7x'.

AD 1897

In Michigan, USA, corn flakes are invented by the Kellogg brothers to feed their fourteen little brothers and sisters.

Taking pictures

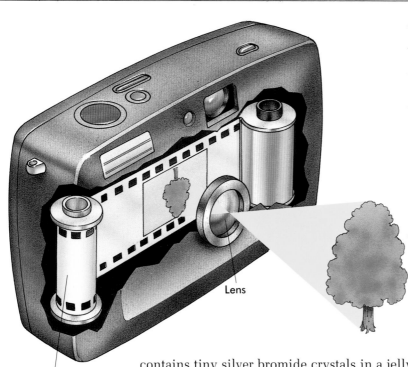

A camera is like your eye. At the front, it has a lens to gather light coming from a scene. An astronomer's telescope uses a large mirror to gather light from distant stars, planets and galaxies.

Lens

Film

Taking a photograph

When you press the shutter release on the camera, the shutter opens for a fraction of a second and light falls on the film. The film is made of celluloid or plastic. One side is coated with a thin layer called an emulsion. The emulsion contains tiny silver bromide crystals in a jelly-like substance called gelatine. The silver bromide crystals are affected by the light that falls on them. To see which crystals have been affected and reveal the image or picture on the film, the film has to be developed.

Developing a film

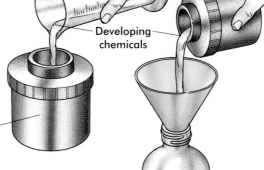

First, the film is wound onto a spool and put inside a light-tight tank. Then the developer is poured in. This is a mixture of chemicals that turn the crystals affected by light into grey or black silver. The more light that has fallen on them, the darker they are.

Spool holding film

Light tight developing tank

Developing chemicals

Rinsing film

This produces a negative image because the parts that should be black are white and vice versa.

Next the film is fixed to make the photographic image permanent. The fixer contains a chemical that washes away all the silver bromide that has not been affected by the light.

All traces of the developing and fixing chemicals are washed away and the film is dried before being printed.

AD 1906

Japanese inventor Satori Kato sells his new invention, instant coffee, in Chicago.

AD 1908

Henry Ford starts to produce the Model T, known as the Tin Lizzie, on a production line. It is the first car to sell by the million.

AD 1909

Leo Baekeland, a Belgian living in America, invents Bakelite, the first artificial plastic.

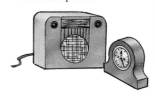

AD 1924

American Clarence Birdseye produces the first frozen food. He had the idea 10 years earlier while hunting in the frozen wastes of Labrador.

INTERNET LINK http://www.kodak.com
Search "box pinhole" and learn how to make a simple camera. You made need an adult's help for this one!

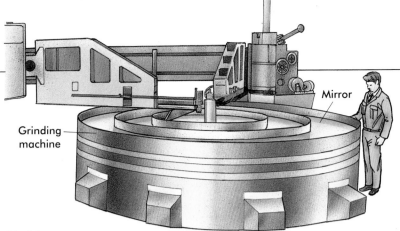

Printing a photograph

The photograph is first enlarged. To do this, the negative is placed in a holder above a lens. The lens focuses a sharp image of the negative on to a board below.

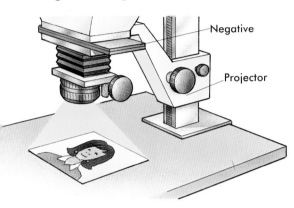

Negative

Projector

A piece of light-sensitive photographic paper is placed on the board. Strong light shone through the negative projects the image on to the paper.

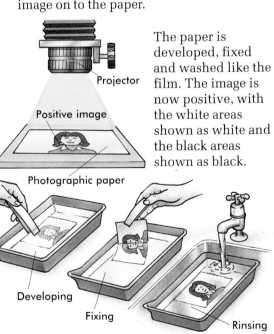

Projector

Positive image

Photographic paper

The paper is developed, fixed and washed like the film. The image is now positive, with the white areas shown as white and the black areas shown as black.

Developing

Fixing

Rinsing

Grinding machine

Mirror

Making a telescope

The mirror of an astronomical telescope is made from a large block of glass. It is shaped into a shallow bowl shape, called a parabola, by a grinding machine. It is very accurately shaped, so the telescope forms a clear image. The perfectly smooth, curved surface of the glass is coated with a layer of aluminium a few millionths of a centimetre thick. This process is carried out in a vacuum by heating some aluminium until it vaporizes. The metal vapour forms a thin reflective layer on the glass surface. The biggest telescope of all is the Keck telescope in Hawaii.

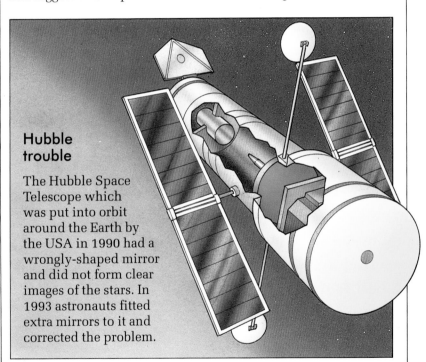

Hubble trouble

The Hubble Space Telescope which was put into orbit around the Earth by the USA in 1990 had a wrongly-shaped mirror and did not form clear images of the stars. In 1993 astronauts fitted extra mirrors to it and corrected the problem.

AD 1926

In Switzerland Hans Wilsdorf makes the first waterproof watch. In 1927 an English typist Mercedes Geitz swims the Channel wearing the watch.

AD 1932

The Empire State Building is erected in New York. It has 102 floors, 6,400 windows and is 448 metres high.

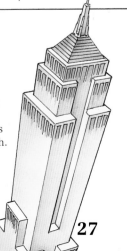

AD 1935

An artificial fibre, nylon, is invented by American chemist Wallace Carothers.

AD 1935

The German firm AEG introduces the first modern tape recorder using plastic tape coated with magnetic particles.

Read all about it!

Before printing was invented, books were copied by hand. This took a long time, so not many books were made. Paper-making and printing began in China. After these processes were rediscovered in Europe, books and newspapers became cheap and plentiful.

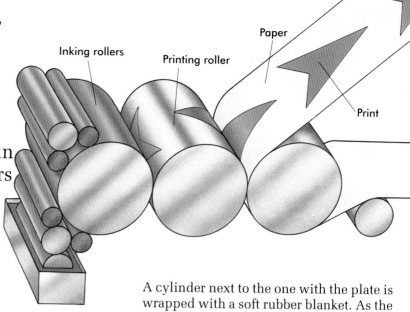

Inking rollers

Printing roller

Paper

Print

Printing books

To make a book like this one, words and pictures are transferred onto thin metal plates using photography. The plate is wrapped around a cylinder and inked by rollers. The ink only sticks on the plate where the words and pictures are.

A cylinder next to the one with the plate is wrapped with a soft rubber blanket. As the cylinder spins, this transfers the ink on to the paper. This process is called lithography.

Making paper

Millions of trees are harvested every year to make paper. Papermaking starts at the pulp mill. First the bark is taken off the tree trunk. Then the wood is chopped into small pieces. These are treated with chemicals to make a pulp, which is washed and bleached. The wood is sometimes mechanically ground up and made into a pulp. The pulp made with chemicals is stronger than paper made mechanically from the wood.

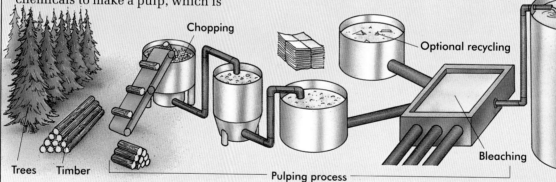

China clay added here

Chopping

Optional recycling

Bleaching

Trees   Timber

Pulping process

AD 1937

The Golden Gate Bridge in San Francisco, California, USA, is completed after four years work.

AD 1938

The Orbig Company in the USA produces the first plastic contact lenses.

AD 1938

The Volkswagen 'Beetle' motorcar is first made in Germany. Now more than 20 million have been made.

AD 1947

The Polaroid Land camera is developed by American Edwin Land. It produces a finished photograph only a few seconds after pressing the button.

INTERNET LINK http://www.mead.com/ml/docs/facts/howmade.html
Discover the secrets behind the paper-making process, and find out how a tree becomes a notebook!

Printing a photograph

To print a photograph, it has to be broken into a pattern of dots, to produce the shades of grey or black. These dots are made by copying the photograph through a fine screen. The picture appears black where black dots cluster together. There are fewer dots in the lighter areas. Pictures made like this are called half-tones.

Colour printing

Four different inks are needed to print colour illustrations. They are yellow, cyan (blue), magenta (red) and black. If you look closely, you can see the coloured dots that make up this picture.

Yellow   Cyan   Magenta   Black

Printed picture

Binding

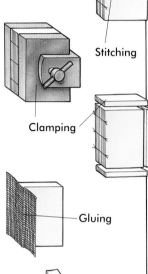

Books are printed on large sheets of paper. The individual pages are arranged so that when each sheet is folded the pages come out in the right order.

Each folded sheet, called a signature, is sewn together. The whole book is firmly clamped and fabric glued to the spine and the book fixed inside its case or cover. The whole process is carried out at high speed by machine.

Signature

Stitching

Clamping

Gluing

Binding

Finished book

The pulp is beaten to separate the wood fibres. Additives such as china clay, whiteners or colour are mixed in at this stage. In the paper-making machine, the slushed pulp is spread out in a thin layer on a moving belt woven from thin wires. Some of the water is removed by rollers before the paper passes on to the drying section of the machine. Here it is squeezed between hot rollers. The new paper is wound into a big roll.

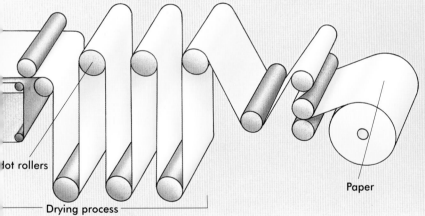

Hot rollers

Drying process

Paper

Papermaking giants

Giant papermaking machines are 75 metres wide. Paper is made at a rate of 900 metres per minute. Water is dried out of the pulp in seconds.

AD 1948

The first LP (long playing) record is produced by Columbia in America.

AD 1959

The front-wheel drive Austin 'Mini' motorcar begins production in Oxford, England.

AD 1960

American Theodor Maiman builds the first laser which produces a thin intense beam of light.

AD 1963

The Dutch firm Philips introduces the cassette recorder which uses cassettes of tape rather than reels.

The sound of music

People made their own music before ways of recording music on discs, records and tapes were invented. Few people ever heard famous musicians and singers performing. Now millions have collections of discs and know exactly what the latest pop group sounds like.

A recording studio

Most pop music recordings are made in a recording studio. Each instrument and voice is recorded separately on tape. This makes it easier to adjust the balance between the instruments and voices, and also allows extra instruments to be added later. This is called dubbing. The musicians perform in a soundproof room. In another room, sound technicians operate the tape machines, amplifiers and sound mixing equipment.

Mixing desk

Monitors (speakers)

Computer screen linked to sequencer

Stereo recording

To listen to a stereo recording you need two loudspeakers or earphones. Each plays a single track recorded on tape or a disc. In a recording session, separate microphones are used to record each instrument and singer. Then before the final record or tape is made the recorded sounds are mixed.

Monitor

Level meters

Faders

Mixing sounds

Sound mixing is an electronic process that blends all the channels recorded in the studio to achieve a good sound. Technicians use a machine called a mixing console which takes all the recorded sounds and produces the final stereo recording on a master tape.

AD 1970

Robots are introduced into car factories in Europe, America and Japan.

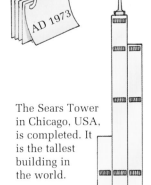

AD 1973

The Sears Tower in Chicago, USA, is completed. It is the tallest building in the world.

AD 1979

Japanese firm Sony markets the first Walkman. It plays stereo cassettes through a pair of lightweight headphones.

Record making

Records are made from the master tape.
First a master disc is made. The sounds are
re-recorded onto an aluminium disc
coated on one side with a black lacquer
using a disc cutting machine. This
machine has a V-shaped ruby or sapphire
cutting stylus. The hot stylus cuts a spiral
groove in the lacquer as the disc rotates.

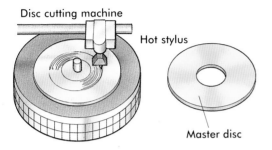

Disc cutting machine

Hot stylus

Master disc

Next, copies of this disc are made. The
copies have a raised track instead of a
spiral groove. These discs are called
stampers.

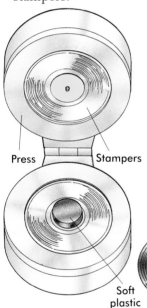

Press   Stampers

The final disc is
made from two
stampers, one for
each side of the
record. A lump of
soft plastic is
placed between the
stampers. The
stampers are
pressed together
briefly and then
opened to release
the record.

Soft
plastic

Making a CD

Making a CD (compact disc) starts with a
round, flat piece of carefully polished
glass. It is coated with a very thin layer of
plastic material, called a photoresist.

A laser fires a very
fine, intense beam
of light at the disc
as it rotates,
producing a spiral
track of minute pits
on the plastic.

Laser forming
master disc

Holes dissolved

The areas of the plastic exposed to the
laser light are now dissolved away,
producing a track on the glass underneath.

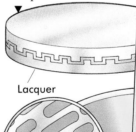

Plastic disc

Stamper (upside down)

A copy of the glass disc, or master, is now
made. On the copy, the minute pits
become projections. These discs are called
stampers and are used to press the CD from
soft plastic.

The transparent plastic disc is coated with
aluminium on one side and protective
lacquer on the other.

The spiral track of a
CD is 5.7 kilometres
long. It would take
about 30 tracks to
cover the width of
a human hair. ▶

Lacquer

Glass

Photoresist layer

Stamper

Small records

The smallest ever
music records were
made in 1923 for
Queen Mary's doll's
house. The records
were only 33
millimetres across.
There were six
different records,
including one of
'God Save the King'.

AD 1981

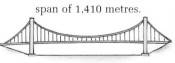

The Humber
suspension bridge
opens in England. It is
the longest single-span
suspension bridge in
the world with a main
span of 1,410 metres.

AD 1982

The CD (compact disc),
developed by Philips
working with Sony, the
Japanese electronics
company, appears. It
soon sells more than
LPs and cassette tapes.

AD 1994

The Channel Tunnel opens. Cars
and trucks travel on a high-speed
train in a double tunnel under the
sea between England and France.

AD 1994

The world's longest
cable-stayed bridge –
the Pont de Normandie
– is completed across
the River Seine, France.
It is 856 metres from
tower to tower.

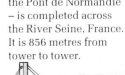

Index